ALL THE COLORS OF ME

PICTURING MY ANGER

KNOWING AND SHOWING MY FEELINGS THROUGH ART

ANNA SHEPHERD
illustrated by ALICIA MÁS

PowerKiDS press

Published in 2027
by The Rosen Publishing Group, Inc.
2544 Clinton Street, Buffalo, NY 14224

First published in Great Britain in 2023 by Hodder & Stoughton

Credits

Series Editor: Grace Glendinning
Series Designer: Alicia Más
Illustrations: Alicia Más

Cataloging-in-Publication Data

Names: Shepherd, Anna, author. | Más, Alicia, illustrator.
Title: Picturing my anger / Anna Shepherd, illustrated by Alicia Más.
Description: Buffalo, New York : PowerKids Press, 2027. | Series: All the colors of me
Identifiers: ISBN 9781499458732 (pbk.) | ISBN 9781499458749 (library bound) | ISBN 9781499458756 (ebook)
Subjects: LCSH: Anger in children--Juvenile literature. | Anger--Juvenile literature. |
Emotions in children--Juvenile literature.
Classification: LCC BF723.A4 S547 2027 | DDC 155.41247--dc23

Printed in China

CPSIA Compliance Information: Batch #QS27PK. For further information contact Rosen Publishing at 1-800-237-9932.

CONTENTS

LISTENING TO ANGER

Anger is normal. Everybody feels mad sometimes.

It is important to hear what our anger is telling us. Anger comes to let us know when things don't feel right or fair.

It can build up or burst out, so knowing what to do with these feelings will really help you day-to-day.

We are often told that anger is not a good thing. But anger is just a feeling. It is **what you do with it** that is important.

What do you USUALLY DO when you feel angry?

Can you remember times in the past when you helped yourself feel a bit better after getting upset?

You can LEARN how to UNDERSTAND this tricky feeling.

ART-MAKING CAN HELP

Doing art can help you understand what is going on inside. This book will show you some ways to give it a go.

When we feel really angry, it can be so tricky to find the words to explain how we feel.

Getting anger out and on to some paper is a great way to **deal with** this feeling before it gets bigger and **BIGGER** and **BIGGER.**

Being creative can show us what we are feeling inside our head and body, and it can show others our big feelings, too.

We are so lucky that we have our imagination. We can really change how we **feel** and **see** things with our fabulous minds!

You might think, "But I'm no good at art!" (Impossible!) But you don't have to worry about what it will look like. It is all about DOING. Then we see how the DOING helps us understand our feelings.

So let's get creative and see what happens!

Making art can help us get to know our anger a bit better. So:

WHAT IS ANGER?

Anger might be a response to something like this ...

... or this.

We might push it down, or it may feel like just too much inside us.

Our anger and others' anger can be scary or confusing. If someone is being angry and you don't feel safe, it is really important that you tell a trusted adult.

We might cry or want to run away.

It helps to picture our anger to get to know it a bit better.

We can start by imagining anger as a shape.

What is it like? Does it fill the whole room? Is it small and spiky? What kind of texture – smooth, sharp, bumpy, or something else?

Now imagine speaking to your anger in a kind and gentle way. How does that feel?

One of the best ways to start spotting anger is to think creatively about what your

ANGER FEELS LIKE.

Can you remember the last time you were angry? Close your eyes.

Try to remember how the anger **felt in your body.**

Did your heart beat **faster**?

Did your muscles feel **weak** or full of **energy**?

Did your body need to **move** or were you **frozen** to the spot?

With this in mind, draw a body shape. Fill it with **all the anger** using colors, shapes, and textures.

Notice which parts of your body feel it most strongly (you can call these your Anger Hot Spots).

Here is mine:

When you are in the middle of anger your brain stops thinking clearly. Exercise can help settle your brain so you can explore how you are feeling.

SOME WAYS TO GET YOUR BODY MOVING!

SWINGING

SPINNING AROUND OUTSIDE

SETTING UP AN OBSTACLE COURSE

JUMPING

After you've moved your body, it can be interesting to go back to a pen and paper! Can you fill another body shape with any new feelings? What new shapes, colors, and textures will you use?

Our art can also help us get to know what our

ANGER LOOKS LIKE

on the **outside.**

Can you pull **your best angry face?**

Have a look in the mirror. Can you make it look even grumpier? Which of the angry faces above does your face most look like?

Think about how your **angry faces** might appear compared to **other emotions.** Why don't you and some friends make different feelings masks and act out a scene using them?

Here are a few things to think about as you prepare your play:

* How will you make your ANGRY mask look really angry?
* What angry colors and features will you use?
* What's going to happen in your play?
* What will the CALM mask do and say?
* What about the WORRIED mask or the SAD one?
* How might they help one another?

Let's think a bit more about what our

ANGER ACTS LIKE.

Everyone feels angry, but how you **behave** when you're angry can be quite different from somebody else.

We don't usually **like** feeling angry. In the moment we might **enjoy** slamming doors, stamping our feet, hitting and shouting, but afterwards it doesn't always feel so good.

It can feel **worrying** when you **lose control** and you might be afraid that you have upset your trusted adults. The great thing is, with a little practice you can try doing it another way next time.

Focusing on your breath gives you a bit of time to stop, slow down and choose what to do next.

Close your eyes and imagine breathing in a lovely calming color. When you breathe out, imagine blowing out all your anger.

Next, grab some paper and make art about what you imagined so you can remember how you dealt with your angry feelings. You can use what you practiced in this meditation to help you steer away from an angry outburst in the future.

Now let's think about noticing some of the different

SHADES OF ANGER

that you might feel.

Here are some great **words** that show anger when it's **little** right up to **HUGE!**

Create an Anger Scale to help you understand how each one is different.

WHAT COLOR WOULD RAGING BE?

RAGING

FURIOUS

BOILING

FUMING

IRRITATED

CROSS

GRUMPY

ANNOYED

HAVE YOU EVER BEEN SO CROSS YOU FEEL LIKE IT IS BOILING UP INSIDE YOU? HOW WOULD YOU DRAW THAT?

WHAT MARKS WOULD YOU MAKE FOR FUMING?

OR IRRITATED?

WHAT COLOR IS A LITTLE BIT CROSS?

Next time you feel somewhere on the angry scale, you can ask yourself: "How angry do I feel? Is it a little bit or quite a lot?"

To practice spotting your shades of anger, fill up a feelings flip book. It can be good to remember how your emotions change.

When you are having a **big feeling** you sometimes think you are going to feel the same **forever**.

Your flip book will remind you how **feelings come and go!**

SPEAKING IN ANGER

can be one of the toughest and most hurtful parts of an angry moment.

When we say things like this or they are said to us it can be **hurtful** or **upsetting**.

With some creativity, we can learn to use helpful words instead, especially if we think them through before we are caught up in anger.

Make yourself a fun cartoon strip filled with excellent words you can use when something makes you angry.

In the middle of an angry moment, you may have no words at all. Try art instead!

Don't think about what you are making – just play with paints or pens. You may be surprised by what your art **says** about your feelings!

What happens when you just

CAN'T STOP THE ANGER?

Sometimes anger can feel **so big** and too difficult to know what to do with.

It can feel like it keeps exploding out and hurting people, making life less enjoyable.

Could there be something underneath the anger?

Remember your feelings masks from page 13? Could it be that another mask might be hiding behind the angry mask?

Can you uncover any other feelings, such as sadness, worry, loneliness, or hurt?

It might also be that, on top of a hard situation, you are hungry or tired or even bored.

Make yourself a Wellness Check poster to hang somewhere you'll see it a lot. If you're struggling to move on from an angry reaction, ask yourself:

IS THERE ANOTHER FEELING HIDING BELOW MY ANGER?

YES --> ASK FOR HELP!

AM I HUNGRY?

YES --> GET A SNACK!

DO I NEED A REST?

YES --> LIE DOWN FOR A WHILE!

ARE MY BODY AND MIND A BIT BORED OR RESTLESS?

YES --> GET UP AND GET MOVING!

IMPORTANT: If you feel that you are stuck in your anger and it all seems too much, it is a good idea to talk to a teacher or someone who is trained to help children with their feelings.

PRACTICING ANGER

means doing even more of what we've just done in this book: spotting when anger is around, realizing what you feel inside, and planning ways to share those feelings.

The more you try things out, the easier it will be next time. Keep practicing and soon you will know just what to do when you are feeling angry.

To help you remember what you learn as you practice, why don't you make a big, colorful sticky-note chart to put on the wall? Keep adding to it and see how much you've learned!

YOU ARE AN ANGER ARTIST!

Making art is a great way to express your feelings. There are so many things you can do along the way to being an expert feelings artist!

You could make something realistic about your anger and include lots of details about it ...

... or something abstract to see what you discover.

You could create a weekly "feelings comic" with friends or on your own. Who will be your main character? What kinds of adventures with emotions will they get up to?

Think about how your favorite cartoon characters show their feelings. How do the cartoonists draw their eyes, their bodies?

Anger might feel like it **fills up your whole body**, so making **big** movements while you are doing your art can help you with these feelings. Experiment and see.

Try jumping around the room before you make each mark.

Pretend to be an angry lion or a hissing snake. What marks would these animals make on the paper?

Get a big roll of paper and splat and splodge paint, and scribble and scrape crayons and pens all over it.

What do you want to do
with your picture?

Do you want anyone to **see** it?
Would it help them to understand
how you feel?

Do you want to **rip** it up,
cut it, and **recycle** it?

Or can you give it a **new purpose**
to help you see it in a new way?

Can you think
of other ways to
make fun art?
I think you have a
BIG imagination,
ready for MANY
shades of anger.

KEY TERMS

Abstract: something that does not look realistic, using shapes, colors, and textures.

Creativity: using your imagination to make something.

Experiment: to try something out without knowing how it will turn out.

Meditation: to focus on your breathing to settle your mind.

Obstacle: something that blocks your way or keeps you from moving forwards.

Realistic: something that looks or feels like the real thing it represents.

Shades: slightly different varieties of something, such as a color.

Texture: the feel or look of the surface of something.

BOOKS TO READ

***Kids Can Cope* series,**
by Gill Hasson (Franklin Watts)

- *Bounce Back from Disappointment*
- *Face Your Fears*
- *Let Go of Jealousy*
- *Put Your Worries Away*
- *Say Hi When You're Shy*
- *Step Back from Frustration*
- *Take Charge of Anger*
- *Turn Away from Teasing*

***A World Full of Feelings* series,**
by Louise Spilsbury (Franklin Watts)

- *Finding Calm*
- *Finding Courage*
- *Finding Happiness*
- *Finding Kindness*

***Build Resilience* series,**
by Honor Head (Franklin Watts)

- *Anxiety and Self-esteem*
- *Coping with Change*
- *Friendships and Bullying*
- *Unexpected Challenges*

WEBSITES to **VISIT** with the help of an adult:

Headspace.com

A website and app offering meditation and mindfulness tools to expand on the practice of understanding and dealing with emotions.

Youthmindfulness.org

Resources for mindfulness programs for young people.

HOW TO USE THIS BOOK: A GUIDE FOR ADULTS

This series of art therapy books has been developed to provide a creative starting point for further discussion and exploration around children's emotions.

Each book is intended for children to **share** with trusted adults, whether one-on-one or in a group setting in the classroom or elsewhere.

This book, *Picturing My Anger*, is a careful exploration of the look and feel of all kinds of anger. When dealing with any tricky emotion, big or small, the utmost priority is making children feel **safe and heard** as they think things through.

Whether sharing at home or in a group setting, plan to begin at a time when you and your child or group are relaxed and have an uninterrupted moment to share an activity. It is important that the adult leading the activity is emotionally available when sitting to do this. This can be hard when you feel rushed and stressed, so choose the timing carefully.

Only you will know how much time and energy you and your child or group are able to give to this practice in each session, and what will suit your setting – dip in; read it completely; return to it again at times in the future. No matter what, **don't push things** – try out the bits that your child or group are most drawn to. Have a go at different activities when they feel right for the progression of the individual or group. Use each approach at a time and place that is **most helpful**.

The activities are catalysts for conversations about how children feel. Once the creativity starts flowing, the session may well grow beyond what's in these pages. Maybe a child has their own ideas about ways to feel a bit better that they could share with you or the group? Try to **listen** and not offer unwelcome solutions or critiques. It can be hard when you want to help, but trust that **with love, support and encouragement,** children can usually find their own way through.

Also, take **notice of your own feelings** and responses as your child or group creates, and be mindful that you are modelling how to manage and regulate emotions. You do not need to get it right all the time; **be kind to yourself**, just as we encourage the children to be throughout this book. Helping children is not always easy.

In a group setting it is very important to make sure every child feels safe to share and participate. Establish a rapport of **support** and **zero judgement** of their art and expression of emotion.

But keep in mind that some children may need to have additional, dedicated help beyond what is appropriate to do on your own in a classroom or group setting. See page 32 for quick-reference contacts if you feel your child or group member needs further professional or anonymous assistance.

If you are concerned that a child is struggling to cope, then it is worth seeking advice from a professional.

American Art Therapy Association
arttherapy.org/art-therapist-locator

Learn more about art therapy and find a trained therapist to continue emotional work with a creative approach.

Find a Warmline
www.warmline.org

Warmlines are confidential, free phone services that offer emotional support to people who just need someone to talk to. Find a Warmline near you here.

Kids Help Phone
1-800-668-6868
kidshelpphone.ca

Kids Help Phone is a Canadian e-mental health service for youths with counselors available 24 hours a day.

National Mental Health Hotline
1-866-903-3787
mentalhealthhotline.org

This free, 24-hour help line connects people in need with caring, knowledgeable, licensed mental health counselors.

Nemours Kids Health
kidshealth.org

This website is full of helpful health resources for parents, kids, teens, and educators.